RELIGION AND ART

IN

ANCIENT GREECE

RELIGION AND ART

IN

ANCIENT GREECE

BY

ERNEST A. GARDNER

YATES PROFESSOR OF ARCHAEOLOGY AND
PUBLIC ORATOR IN THE UNIVERSITY OF
LONDON ; LATE DIRECTOR OF THE BRITISH
SCHOOL AT ATHENS

KENNIKAT PRESS
Port Washington, N. Y./London

RELIGION AND ART IN ANCIENT GREECE

First published in 1910
Reissued in 1969 by Kennikat Press
Library of Congress Catalog Card No: 77-101041
SBN 8046-0707-9

Manufactured by Taylor Publishing Company   Dallas, Texas

KENNIKAT CLASSICS SERIES

PREFACE

GREEK religion may be studied under various aspects ; and many recent contributions to this study have been mainly concerned either with the remote origin of many of its ceremonies in primitive ritual, or with the manner in which some of its obscurer manifestations met the deeper spiritual needs which did not find satisfaction in the official cults. Such discussions are of the highest interest to the anthropologist and to the psychologist ; but they have the disadvantage of fixing our attention too exclusively on what, to the ordinary Greek, appeared accidental or even morbid, and of making us regard the Olympian pantheon, with its clearly realised figures of the gods, as a mere system imposed more or less from outside upon the old rites and beliefs of the people. In the province of art, at least, the Olympian gods are paramount ; and thus we are led to appreciate and to understand their worship as it affected the religious ideals of the people and the services of the State. For we must remember that, in the case of religion even more than in that of art, its essential character and its influence upon life and thought lie rather in its full perfection than in its origin.

In a short sketch of so wide a subject it has seemed inadvisable to make any attempt to describe the types of the various gods. Without full illustration and a considerable expenditure of space, such a description would be impracticable, and the reader must be referred to the ordinary handbooks of the subject. A fuller account will be found in Dr. Farnell's *Cults of the Greek States*, and some selected types are discussed with the greatest subtlety and understanding in Brunn's

PREFACE

Griechische Götterideale. In the present volume only a few examples are mentioned as characteristic of the various periods. It may thus, I trust, serve as an introduction to a more complete study of the subject ; and may, at the same time, offer to those who have not the leisure or inclination for such further study, at least a summary of what we may learn from Greece as to the relations of religion and art under the most favourable conditions. It is easy, as Aristotle says, to fill in the details if only the outlines are rightly drawn—δόξειε δ' ἂν παντὸς εἶναι προαγαγεῖν καὶ διορθῶσαι τὰ καλῶς ἔχοντα τῇ περιγραφῇ.

CONTENTS

RELIGION AND ART IN ANCIENT GREECE

CHAPTER I

INTRODUCTION — IDOLATRY AND IMAGINATION

THE relation of religion to art has varied greatly among different peoples and at different periods. At the one extreme is the uncompromising puritan spirit, which refuses to admit any devices of human skill into the direct relations between God and man, whether it be in the beauty of church or temple, in the ritual of their service, or in the images which they enshrine. Other religions, such as those of the Jews or of Islam, relegate art to a subordinate position ; and while they accept its services to decorate the buildings and apparatus connected with divine worship, forbid any attempt to make a visible representation

B

of the deity. Modern Christianity, while it does not, as a rule, repeat this prohibition, has varied greatly from time to time and from country to country as to the extent to which it allows such representations. Probably the better educated or more thoughtful individuals would in every case regard them merely as symbolic aids to induce the concentration and intensity of religious ideas and aspirations ; but there is no doubt that among the common people they tend to become actually objects of worship in themselves. It is instructive to turn to a system in which idolatry, the worship of images, was an essential part of orthodox religious observance. It is easy and customary with a certain class of minds to dismiss all such examples of idolatry with a superficial generalisation such as " the heathen in his blindness bows down to stock and stone." But it seems worth while to devote a short study to an attempt to understand how such a system worked in the case

2

of a people like the ancient Greeks, who possessed to a degree that has never been surpassed both clearness of intellectual perception and a power to embody their ideals in artistic form. Whether it tended to exalt or to debase religion may be a doubtful question ; but there can be no doubt that it gave an inspiration to art which contributed to the unrivalled attainments of the Greeks in many branches of artistic creation. We shall be mainly concerned here with the religion of Greece as it affected the art of sculpture ; but before attempting a historical summary it is necessary for us to understand exactly what we mean by the worship of representations of the gods, and to consider the nature of the influence which such representation must have upon artistic activity.

Idolatry—the worship of images—is almost always used by us in a bad sense, owing, no doubt, chiefly to the usage of the word in the Jewish scriptures. Mr. Ruskin, in his chapter on the subject in his *Aratra Pentelici*, points out that it may also be used in a good sense, though he prefers to use the word imagination in this meaning. There is doubtless a frequent tendency to failure to

" Look through the sign to the thing signified,"

but there is no essential reason why the contemplation of a beautiful statue, embodying a worthy conception of the deity, should not be as conducive to a state of worship and communion as is an impressive ritual or ceremony, or any other aid to devotion. This view of the matter is expressed by some later Greek writers ; in earlier times it was probably unconsciously present, though it is hardly to be found in contemporary literature. But it was only by slow stages that art came to do so direct a service to religious ideas ; in more primitive times its relation was more subordinate. The worship or service of images, even in

4

the highest ages of Greek civilisation, was much more associated with primitive and comparatively inartistic figures than with the masterpieces of sculpture ; and even where these masterpieces were actually objects of worship it was often from the inheritance of a sanctity transferred to them from an earlier image rather than for their own artistic qualities. It does not, indeed, follow that the influence of the great sculptors upon the religious ideals of the people was a negligible quality ; we have abundant evidence, both direct and indirect, that it was very great. But it was exercised chiefly by following and ennobling traditional notions rather than by daring innovation, and therefore can only be understood in relation to the general development both of religious conceptions and of artistic facility.

Here we shall be mainly concerned with art as an expression of the religious ideals and aspirations of the people, and as an

influence upon popular and educated opin-
ions and conceptions of the gods. But we
must not forget that it is also valuable to
us as a record of myths and beliefs, and
of ritual and customs associated with the
worship of the gods. This is the case, above
all, with reliefs and vase-paintings. In them
we often find representations which do not
merely illustrate ancient literature, but sup-
plement and modify the information we
derive from classical writers. The point of
view of the artist is often not the same as
that of the poet or historian, and it is frequently nearer to that of the people, and
therefore a help in any attempt to understand popular beliefs. The representations
of the gods which we find in such works do
not often embody any lofty ideals or subtle
characterisation ; but they show us the
traditional and easily recognisable figures in
which the gods usually occurred to the
imagination of the Greek people.

The association of acts of worship with

6

certain specially sacred objects or places
lies at the basis of much religious art,
though very often art has little or nothing
to do with such objects in a primitive stage
of religious development. Stocks and stones
—the latter often reputed to have fallen
from heaven, the former sometimes in the
shape of a growing tree, sometimes of a
mere unwrought log—were to be found as
the centres of religious cult in many of the
shrines of Greece. These sacred objects are
sometimes called fetishes ; and although it
is perhaps wiser to avoid terms belonging
properly to the religion of modern savages
in speaking of ancient Greece, there seems
to be an analogy between the beliefs and
customs that are implied. Such sacred
stocks or stones were not regarded merely
as symbols of certain deities, but were
looked upon as having certain occult or
magic qualities inherent in them, and as
being in themselves potent for good or evil.
The ceremonies used in their cult partook

of the nature of magic rather than religion, so far as these consisted of anointing them with oil or with drink offerings ; such ceremonies might, indeed, be regarded as gratifying to the deity worshipped under their form, when they were definitely affiliated to the service of an anthropomorphic god ; but in a more primitive stage of belief the indwelling power probably was not associated with any such generalisation as is implied in the change from " animism " or " polydæmonism " to polytheism. We are here concerned not with this growth of religious feeling, but rather with its influence upon the sacred things that were objects of worship and with the question how far their sanctity encouraged their artistic decoration.

It is perhaps easier to realise the feeling of a primitive people about this matter in the case of a sacred building than in that of the actual image of a god. A temple does not, indeed — in Greece, at

least—belong to the earliest phase of cult ;
for it is the dwelling of the god, and its
form, based on that of a human dwelling-
house, implies an anthropomorphic imagination. We find, however, in Homer that
the gods are actually thought of as in-
habiting their temples and preferring one
to another, Athena going to Athens and
Aphrodite to Paphos as her chosen abode.
It was clearly desirable for every city to
gain this special favour ; and an obvious
way to do this was to make the dwelling-
place attractive in itself to the deity. This
might be done not merely by the abundance
of sacrifices, but also by the architectural
beauty of the building itself, and by the
richness of the offerings it contained. Here
was, therefore, a very practical reason
for making the dwelling of the god as
sumptuous and beautiful as possible, in order
that he might be attracted to live in it and
to give his favour and protection to those
that dwelt around it. Doubtless, as re-

ligious ideas advanced and the conception of the nature of the gods became higher, there came the notion that they did not dwell in houses made with hands; yet a Greek temple, just like a mediæval cathedral, might be made beautiful as a pleasing service and an honour to the deity to whom it was dedicated; and there was a continuous tradition in practice from the lower conception to the higher, nor is it easy to draw the line at any particular stage between the two.

If we turn now to the sacred image of the deity we find the same process going on. The rude stock or stone was sometimes itself the actual recipient of material offerings; or it might be painted with some bright and pleasing colour, or wrapped in costly draperies. In most of these customs an assumption is implied that the object of worship is pleased by the same things as please its worshippers; and here we find the germ of the anthropomorphic idea. It was probably the desire to make the offerings and prayers of the worshippers perceptible to the power within that first led to the addition of human features to the shape-less block. Just as the early Greeks painted eyes upon the prows of their ships, to enable them to find their way through the water, so they carved a head, with eyes and ears, out of the sacred stone or stock, or perhaps added a head to the original shapeless mass. We find many primitive idols in this form—a cone or column with a head and perhaps arms and feet added to it ; and the tradi-tion survives in the herm, or in the mask of Dionysus attached to a post, round which we still see the Mænads dancing on fifth-century vases. The notion that such carved eyes or ears actually served to transmit im-pressions to the god is well illustrated by Professor Petrie's discovery at Memphis of a number of votive ears of the god, intended to facilitate or to symbolise his reception of the prayers of his votaries. In fact, the

11

taunt of the psalmist against the images of the heathen—" Eyes have they, but they see not ; they have ears, and yet they hear not "—is not a merely rhetorical one, as it seems to us, but real and practical, if spoken to men who gave their gods ears and eyes that they might hear and see.

An imagination so entirely materialistic may belong to a more primitive stage than any we can find among the Greeks. As soon as religion has reached the polytheistic stage the gods are regarded as travelling from image to image, just as they travel from temple to temple. Even in Æschylus' *Eumenides* it will be remembered that when Orestes, by the advice of Apollo, clasps as a suppliant the ancient image of Athena at Athens, the goddess comes flying from far away in the Troad when she hears the sound of his calling. The exact relation of the goddess to the image is not, in all probability, very clearly realised ; but, so far as one can trace it from the ritual procedure,

what appears to be implied is that a suppliant will have a better chance of reaching
the deity he addresses if he approaches one
of the images preferred by that deity as the
abode of his power ; often there is one such
image preferred to all others, as this early
one of Athena at Athens. The deity was
not, therefore, regarded as immanent in any
image—at least, in classical times ; the gods
lived in Olympus, or possibly visited from
time to time the people whom they favoured,
or went to the great festivals that were held
in their honour. But the various images of
them, especially the most ancient ones, that
were set up in their temples in the various
cities of Greece were regarded as a means
of communication between gods and men.
The prayer of a worshipper addressing such
an image will be transmitted to the deity
whom he addresses, and the deity may even
come in person to hear him, if special aid is
required. A close parallel may be found
even in modern days. I have known of a

child, brought up in the Roman Catholic religion, who had a particular veneration or affection for a certain statue of the Virgin, and used often to address it or, as she said, converse with it. And she said she had an impression that, if only she could slip in unawares, she might see the Virgin Mary herself approaching or leaving the statue, whether to be transformed into it or merely to dwell in it for a time. On Greek vases we see the same notion expressed as in the *Eumenides*, when a god or goddess is represented as actually present beside the statue to which a sacrifice or prayer is being offered.

In such a stage of religious belief or imagination it is clearly of high importance that the image of any deity should be pleasing to that deity, and thereby attract his presence and serve as a ready channel of communication with him. From the point of view of art, it would seem at first sight that the result would be a desire to make the image

14

as beautiful as possible, and as worthy an embodiment of the deity as the sculptor could devise. This doubtless was the result in the finest period of art in Greece, and it involved, as we shall see, a great deal of reciprocal influence on the part of religion and art. But in earlier times the case is not so simple ; and even in statues of the fifth century it is not easy to understand the conditions under which the sculptor worked without some reference to the historical development that lay behind him.

Before the rise of sculpture in Greece, images of the gods, some of them only rudely anthropomorphic, had long been objects of worship ; and it was by no means safe in religious matters to depart too rashly from the forms consecrated by tradition. This was partly owing to the feeling that when a certain form had been accepted, and a certain means of communication had worked for a long time satisfactorily, it was a dangerous thing to make a change which

might not be agreeable to the powers concerned, and which might, so to speak, break
the established connection. But while
hieratic conservatism tended to preserve
forms and formulæ almost for what we may
call magic reasons, there was also a sentiment about the matter which gave popular
support to the tendency. Thus Pausanias
probably expresses a common feeling when
he says that the images made by Dædalus,
" though somewhat strange in aspect, yet
seem to be distinguished by something in
them of the divine."

It is true that these early images attributed to Dædalus showed already a considerable advance on the shapeless or
roughly shaped stocks or stones that had
served as the most primitive objects of
worship ; but it was their resemblance to
these rather than their difference from them
that impressed the imagination of Pausanias. He appreciated them not so much
as examples of an art that promised much

for the future, but rather as linked with the past by the tradition of an immemorial sanctity. We find, in fact, that the rude early images remained the centres of state cult and official worship, as well as of popular veneration, long after the art of sculpture had become capable of providing their worshippers with more adequate embodiments of the gods they represented. It was the early image of Athena, not the Athena Parthenos by Phidias, that was annually washed in the sea, and for which the peplos was woven by the chosen women of Athens. The connection between art and religion is, in such a case, reduced to narrow limits ; but, on the other hand, we hear of many instances where new statues of the gods were made as temple statues, to be the chief objects of worship and centres of cult. And this was sometimes done with the official sanction of the gods themselves, as expressed through the oracle of Delphi.

The sanctity of the old image was sometimes transferred to the new one ; a striking example of this is seen in the case of Artemis Brauronia on the Athenian Acropolis. It had been the custom for the garments presented to the goddess by her worshippers to be placed upon her primitive statue ; and when a new and worthier representation of the goddess was placed in the temple in the fourth century, we are informed by inscriptions that dedicated garments were sometimes hung upon it, even though it was a statue from the hand of Praxiteles. It sometimes happened that the old and the new statues stood side by side in the same temple, or in adjacent temples, and they seem then to exemplify the two kinds of idolatry—the literal and the imaginative—the one being the actual subject of the rites ceremonially observed, and the other being the visible presentment of the deity, and helping the worshipper to concentrate his prayers and aspirations. Here the art of the sculptor had the fullest scope, and it is in such cases that he could, as Quintilian said of Phidias, "make some addition to the received religion."

This duality was, however, the result of accident rather than the normal arrangement, and, so long as the primitive image remained the official object of worship, it was difficult, if not impossible, for the new and more artistic statue to have its full religious effect. In many cases, probably in most cases, it was actually substituted, sooner or later, for the earlier embodiment of the deity. Sometimes the early image, which was often of wood, may have decayed or been worn away by the attentions lavished upon it ; we hear of a statue of which the hand had perished under the kisses of the devout. We hear also of cases in which it had been entirely lost—for instance, the Black Demete of Phigalia, an uncouth image with a horse's head ; here, when a plague had warned the people to replace it, the Æginetan sculptor Onatas

undertook the task ; and he is said to have
been vouchsafed a vision in sleep which
enabled him to reproduce exactly this un-
sightly idol. It would not seem that such a
commission gave much scope to his artistic
powers ; but it is noteworthy that the Phi-
galians employed one of the most famous
sculptors of the day. Elsewhere the conditions were more favourable, and it was
possible for the artist, while conforming to
the accepted type, to give it a more correct
form and more pleasing features.

Dædalus, we are told—and in this story
Dædalus is an impersonation of the art of
the early sculptors in Greece—made statues
of the gods so life-like that they had to be
chained to their pedestals for fear they
should run away. It is likely that this tale
goes back to a genuine tradition ; for Pausanias actually saw statues with fetters
attached to them in several early shrines in
Greece. The device is natural enough.
Dædalus was a magician as well as a sculp-

tor ; and if he could give his statues eyes
that they might see, and ears that they
might hear, it was an obvious inference
that if he gave them legs they might run
away and desert their shrines and their
worshippers.

We may very likely find also in a similar
notion the explanation of a peculiarity
often found in early statues of the gods—the
well-known archaic smile. Many explana-
tions, technical and otherwise, have been
given of this device ; but none of them can
get over the fact that it was just as easy, or
even easier, for a primitive sculptor to make
the mouth straight as to make it curve up
at the ends, and that he often did make it
straight. When he does not do so, it is probably done with intention ; and it is quite
in accordance with the conditions of early
religious art that he should make the image
of a deity smile in order that the deity
himself might smile upon his worshippers ;
and a pleasant expression might also, by a

natural transfer of ideas, be supposed to be pleasing to the god, and so attract him to his statue. We are told that at Chios there was a head of Artemis set high up, which appeared morose to those entering the temple, but when they left it seemed to have become cheerful. This may have been originally due to some accident of placing or lighting, but it seems to have acquired a religious significance ; and we can hardly deny a similar significance to the smile which we find on so many early statues. In some cases, especially in statues of men, it may have been intended merely as a device to give expression and life to the face ; but it cannot have been a matter of indifference to a primitive worshipper that his deity should smile on him through the face of its visible image. This point of view being given, it is evidently only a question of how far it is within the power of art to express the benignity of the god, and later on his character and personality, in an adequate manner ; and this power depends on the gradual acquisition of mastery over form and material, of knowledge and observation of the human body and face, and of the technical skill requisite to express this knowledge in marble or bronze, or more precious materials such as gold and ivory. All this development belongs to the history of art, not to that of religion. But before we can pursue the investigation any further, it is necessary to consider the different sources and channels of religious influence on art with which we have to deal.

CHAPTER II

VARIOUS ASPECTS OF RELIGION

RELIGION, for our present purpose, may be considered as (1) popular, (2) official, (3) poetic, and (4) philosophical. These four divisions, or rather aspects, are not, of course, mutually exclusive, and they act and react extensively upon one another ; but, in their relations to art, it is convenient to observe the distinction between them.

(1) The beliefs of the people are, of course, the basis of all the others, though they come to be affected by these others in various degrees. There is no doubt that the people generally believed in the sanctity and efficacy of the shapeless idols or primitive images, and this belief would tend to support hieratic conservatism, and thus to hinder artistic progress. But, on the other

hand, the people of Greece showed throughout their history a tendency to an intensely
and vividly anthropomorphic imagination.
This tendency was doubtless realised and
encouraged by the poets, but it was not
created by them, any more than by the
mythologists who defined and systematised
it. The exact relation of this anthropomorphic imagination to the primitive sacred
stocks and stones is not easy to ascertain ;
but it seems to have tended, on the one
hand, to the realisation of the existence of
the gods apart from such sacred objects,
and thus to reduce the stocks and stones to
the position of symbols—a great advance in
religious ideals ; and, on the other hand, to
the transformation of the stocks and stones
into human form, not merely by giving
them ears and eyes that they might hear
and see, but also by making them take the
image and character of the deity whom they
represented.

It was impossible for any ordinary Greek

to think of the gods in other than human form. He had, indeed, no such definite dogma as the Hebrew statement that " God created man in His own image "; for the legends about the origin of the human race varied considerably, and many of them represented crude philosophical theorising rather than religious belief. But the monstrous forms which we find in Egypt and Mesopotamia as embodiments of divine power were alien to the Greek imagination ; if we find here and there a survival of some strange type, such as the horse-headed Demeter at Phigalia, it remains isolated and has little influence upon prevalent beliefs. The Greek certainly thought of his gods as having the same human form as himself ; and not the gods only, but also the semi-divine, semi-human, sometimes less than human beings with which his imagination peopled the woods and mountains and seas. His Nereids had human feet, not fishy tails like our mer-

maids ; and if centaurs and satyrs and some
other creatures of his imagination showed
something of the beast within the man in
their visible shape, they had little about
them of the mysterious or the unearthly.
It would be a great mistake to regard all
these creatures as mere impersonations or
abstractions. If " a pagan suckled in a
creed outworn " could

> " Have sight of Proteus coming from the sea
> And hear old Triton blow his wreathed horn,"

much more were such sights and sounds
familiar to his forefathers, to whom the
same beliefs were fresh and real. Even to
the present day Greek peasants may often
be found who can tell of such experiences ;
to them, as to the Greeks of old, desert
places and remote woods and mountains are
terrible, not because they are lonely, but
because when a man is alone then is he
least alone ; hence the panic terror, the
terror of Pan.

The same idea, which later takes the religious or philosophic form of the belief in the omnipresence of the deity, peopled the woods with dryads, the streams and springs with nymphs and river-gods, the seas with Nereids and Tritons. When an artist represented a mountain or a river-god, a nymph or a Triton, or added such figures to a scene to indicate its locality by what seems to us at first sight a mere artistic convention, he was not inventing an impersonation, but he was representing something which, in the imagination of the people, might actually be seen upon the spot—at least, by those whose eyes were opened to see it. It was the same gift of imagination that made Blake say : " ' What,' it will be questioned, ' when the sun rises, do you not see a disc of fire, somewhat like a guinea ? ' ' Oh no, no ! I see an innumerable company of the heavenly host, crying " Holy, holy, holy is the Lord God Almighty ! " I question not my corporeal eye, any more than I would question a window, concerning a sight. I look through it, and not with it.' " *

In the case of the gods, the matter is somewhat less simple than in that of all these dæmonic creatures of the popular imagination. Gods imply a greater power of generalisation and a higher stage of religious development. It was not thought likely that the gods would show themselves to mortal eyes, as had been their habit in the Golden Age, except perhaps upon some occasion of a great national crisis ; and even then it was the heroes rather than the gods who manifested themselves. But the ordinary Greek believed that the gods actually existed in human form, and even that their characters and passions and moods were like those of human beings. The influence of the poet and the artist could not have been so vigorous if it had not found, in the imagination of the people, a suitable and sympathetic material.

* Blake, "Aldine" edition, p. cvi.

(2) Official or state religion consisted in the main of an organisation of popular ritual. There was no priestcraft in Greece, no exclusive caste to whom the worship of the gods was assigned, although, of course, the right to practise certain cults belonged to particular families. But a priesthood, as a rule, was a political office like any other magistracy, and there was no exclusive tradition in the case of the chief cults of any Greek state to keep the point of view of the priests different from that of the people generally. The tendency of state religion was, as a rule, conservative, for reasons that we have already noticed; innovations in the matter of ritual are dangerous, for the new rite may not please the gods as well as the old; and the same feeling applies to the statues that form the centres of ritual. Pericles, for example, doubtless wished to make the Athena Parthenos of Phidias the official and visible representation of the goddess of Athens, and thereby to raise the

religious ideals of the Athenians. In this last part of his attempt he was successful ; the statue became the pride and glory of the city in its fitting shrine, the Parthenon ; but the old image was still preserved in the temple of Athena Polias, and remained the official centre of worship. We are not told that Pericles meant to supersede it ; but it is very probable that he intended to do so, and was only prevented by the religious conservatism that curtailed other plans of his for the beautifying of the Acropolis. On the other hand, there is no evidence that in Greece—at least, in the best period of Greek art—any statesman held the views as to the official religion frankly expressed in Rome, that it was expedient for this religion to be accepted by the common people, but that educated men could only reconcile their consciences to taking part in it by a philosophical interpretation.

There is something unreal and artificial

about any such compromise. If Pericles was intimate with Anaxagoras, who was prosecuted for atheism, he was also the friend of Phidias, who expressly said that his Zeus was the Zeus of Homer, no mere abstract ideal of divinity. If this was the case with Pericles, who held himself aloof from the common people, it must have been much more so with other statesmen, who mingled with them more freely, or even, like Nicias, shared their superstitions. Under such conditions the influence of art upon the representations of the gods could not well go in advance of popular conceptions, though it might accompany and direct them. The making of new statues of the gods, to be set up as the centres of worship in their temples, in some cases received the formal sanction of the Delphic oracle, the highest official and religious authority. Public commissions of this sort are common at all times, but commonest in the years immediately succeeding the Persian Wars, when the spoils of the Persians supplied ample resources, and in many cases the ancient temples and images had been destroyed ; and at the same time the outburst of national enthusiasm over the great deliverance led to a desire to give due thankofferings to the gods of the Hellenic race, a desire which coincided with the ability to fulfil it, owing to the rapid progress of artistic power. Such public commissions, and the popular feeling which they expressed, offered an inspiration to the artist such as has rarely, if ever, found a parallel. But any great victory or deliverance might be commemorated by the setting up of statues of the gods to whom it was attributed ; and in this way the demands of official religion offered the sculptor the highest scope for the exercise of his art and his imagination.

(3) The influence of poetic mythology upon art can hardly be exaggerated. The statement of Herodotus that Homer and

Hesiod " made the Greek theogony, and assigned to the gods their epithets and distinguished their prerogatives and their functions, and indicated their form," would not, of course, be accepted in a literal sense by any modern mythologist. But it is nevertheless true that the clear and vivid personality and individuality given to the gods by the epic poets affects all later poetry and all Greek art. The imagination of the poets could not, as we have already noticed, have had so deep and wide an influence unless it had been based upon popular beliefs and conceptions. But it fills these conceptions with real and vivid character, so that the gods of Homer are as clearly presented to us as any personalities of history or fiction. They are, indeed, endowed not only with the form, but with the passions, and some even of the weaknesses of mankind ; and for this reason the philosophers often rejected as unworthy the tales that the poets told of the gods. But even an artist such as Phidias expressly stated that it was the Zeus of Homer who inspired his greatest work, quoting the well-known passage in the Iliad in which the god grants the prayer of Thetis :—

" He said ; and his black eyebrows bent; above his
        deathless head
    Th' ambrosian curls flowed ; great heaven shook."

Descriptive passages such as this are not, indeed, common, because, as Lessing clearly pointed out, the poet depends more upon action and its effect than on mere enumerative description. Even here it is the action of the nod, and the shaking of heaven that follows it, that emphasises the impression, rather than the mere mention of eyebrows or hair. In many other cases the distinctive epithet has its value for all later art—the cow-eyed Hera, the grey-eyed Athena, the swift messenger Hermes ; but, above all, it is the action and character of the various gods that is so clearly realised by the poet that his successors cannot, if they wish, escape from his spell.

The influence of the various Greek poets is not, indeed, for the most part, to be traced in contemporary Greek art. This is obvious in the case of the Homeric poems, for the art of the time was of a purely decorative character, and was quite incapable of representing in any adequate way the vivid and lively imagination of the poets; and, for that matter, for many centuries after the date of the composition of the Iliad and Odyssey, Hellenic art made no attempt to cope with any so ambitious problems. Even when the art of sculpture had attained to a considerable degree of mastery over material and expression, we find its aims and conceptions lagging far behind those of the poet. This will become clearer when, in the next chapter, we consider the conditions of artistic expression in Greece; but it must be noted here, in order to prevent possible misconception. As soon, however, as art became capable of aiming at something beyond perfection of bodily form —a change which, in spite of Pausanias' admiration of something divine about the works of Dædalus, can hardly be dated earlier than the fifth century B.C.—the Homeric conceptions of the gods came to have their full effect. Zeus, the king and father of gods and men ; Athena, the friendly protectress of heroes, irresistible in war, giver of all intellectual and artistic power ; Apollo, the archer and musician, the purifier and soothsayer—these and others find their first visible embodiment in the statues whereby the sculptors of the fifth century gave expression to the Homeric conceptions.

The tales, too, that were told about the gods, some of them trivial enough, but others full of religious and ethical significance, had for some time before this been common subjects upon reliefs and vase-paintings, and on these also the influence of the poets was very great. Here we have not only the Iliad and Odyssey to consider, but many other early epics that are now lost to us. The vase-painter or sculptor did not, indeed, merely illustrate these stories as a modern artist might ; often he had a separate tradition and a repertory of subjects belonging to his own art, and developed them along different lines from those followed by the poets. But although this tradition might lead him to choose a version less familiar to poetry, or even to give a new form to an old story, his conception was essentially poetical, in that it implied an imaginative realisation of the scene or action, and even of the character of the deity or hero represented.

The conception of the gods to be found in other early epics probably did not differ essentially from that we find in the Iliad and Odyssey ; but with the Homeric hymns and with some of the earlier lyric poets we find a change setting in. There seems to be a new interest in the adventures of the gods themselves, apart from their relation to mankind ; romantic and even pathetic stories are told about them, implying almost a psychological appreciation of their personality—the tale of Demeter's mourning for her daughter Persephone, her wanderings and adventures ; of the love of Aphrodite for a mortal ; of how Hermes invented the lyre and tricked Apollo about his cattle ; of the birth of Apollo and the founding of his worship at Delos and Delphi ; of the marvellous birth of Athena from the head of Zeus. It is hardly too much to say that in the later of these Homeric hymns—those that are mentioned first in the above enumeration—an almost human interest is given to the gods, to their sufferings and adventures. It is the same tendency which we see in the lyric poetry of the Greeks, with its intensely personal note. The reflexion of this tendency in art is not, indeed, to be seen until the fourth century ; not only the power of expression, but the desire to express such a side of the character of the gods seems to be absent until this period.

It may seem curious at first sight that art was so slow in this case to follow the lead given it by poetry ; but it is to be remembered that a power of expression such as would have enabled it to do so was not attained until the fifth century, and that in this age there was an exaltation of national and religious enthusiasm, owing mainly to the victories over the Persians, which checked the tendency to sentiment and pathos ; and it was not until this vigorous reaction had died away that the tendency once more asserted itself. The early fifth century was also marked by poets such as Pindar and Æschylus, who raised the religious ideals of the nation on to a higher plane, who consciously rejected the less worthy conceptions of the gods, and, whether in accordance with the popular beliefs or not, gave expression to a higher truth in religion than had hitherto been dreamed of. The gods whom the sculptors of the fifth century were called upon to represent may have been the gods of Homer, but they were the Homeric gods transformed by the creative imagination of a more reflective age, and purified by a poetic, if not a philosophic, idealism. But while Æschylus suggests " a deeply brooding mind, tinged with mysticism, grappling with dark problems of life and fate," * and so was, in some ways, remote from the clarity and definition of sculptural form, Sophocles " invests the conceptions of popular religion with a higher spiritual and intellectual meaning ; and the artistic side of the age is expressed by him in poetry, much as in architecture and sculpture it is interpreted by the remains of the Parthenon ; there is the same serenity and wholeness of

* Sir R. C. Jebb in *Cambridge Companion to Greek Studies*, p. 110.

work ; power joined to purity of taste ; self-restraint ; and a sure instinct of symmetry." * Sophocles was a friend and companion of Pericles, and therefore probably of Phidias ; and in both alike we see the same harmony and absence of exaggeration that are characteristic of Greek art at its best. In this case we may say with some confidence that the poet and the sculptor probably influenced each other.

It seems a tempting hypothesis to see something of the influence of "Euripides the human" in the individualistic tendencies of the art of the fourth century ; but it seems hardly to be justified by the facts. The influence of his dramas is, indeed, to be seen in later vase-paintings ; but this is not a matter with which we are here concerned. In his treatment of the gods, Euripides can hardly be quoted as an example of the humanising tendency. "He resented the notion that gods could be un-

* *Ibid.* p. 113.

just or impure "; but the purer and more
abstract conceptions of divinity that appealed to him were hardly such as could find
expression in art; it has even been said
that "he blurred those Hellenic ideals
which were the common man's best without
definitely replacing them." The bringing
of these ideals nearer to the common life of
man finds its poetic inspiration rather in the
tendency which has already been noticed in
the Homeric hymns and the lyric poets, and
which now, after the reaction of the fifth
century, exerts its full force on the art of
Scopas and Praxiteles.

There is no need to dwell here on the influence of later poets upon religious art,
though we shall have to notice hereafter the
parallel development of the representation
of the gods in Hellenistic sculpture. The
Alexandrian poets expressed in elegant language their learning on matters of religion
and mythology, but there was no living
belief in the subjects which they made their

theme; and the art they inspired could only show the same qualities of a correct and academic eclecticism. The idylls of Theocritus find, indeed, a parallel in the playful treatment of Satyrs and other subjects of a similar character; but these belong to what may be called mythological genre rather than to religious art. The dramatic vigour and intensity which we find in the art of Pergamon cannot easily be traced to the influence of any similar development in literature, though its artificial and learned mythology is such as we find also in the work of Hellenistic poets.

(4) The philosophical aspect of religion had no very great influence upon art in Greece. We might perhaps expect that, so far as the philosophers accepted the popular religion, they would tend to purify it and to give it a higher meaning, just as the more thoughtful of the poets doubtless assisted the idealising tendency of fifth-century art. And it might well seem that, for example,

Plato's theory of ideas supplies a more satisfactory basis for an idealist art than any other system, since it might be maintained that the true artist represents not the material object which he sees before him, but the ideal prototype of which it is but a faint and inadequate reflexion. This theory is peculiarly applicable to statues of the gods, and we find it so applied by later philosophical and rhetorical writers ; for instance, Cicero says that Phidias " when he was making the statue of Zeus or of Athena did not derive his image from some individual, but within his own mind there was a perfect ideal of beauty ; and gazing on this and in contemplation of it, he guided the craft of his hand after its likeness." *
The same notion underlies the saying quoted by Strabo, that Phidias was " either the only man that saw, or the only man that revealed to others the images of the gods." †

* *Or.* 2. 8.
† viii. p. 353. It does not matter whether the passage is quoted by Strabo himself or by an interpolator.

But there is no trace or encouragement of
any such feeling in the philosophic literature
contemporary with the great age of Greek
art. Plato expressly states that the artist
only makes " an imitation of an imitation " ;
and the higher ideas of divinity preached by
philosophers did not so much tend to en-
noble the popular conceptions as to substi-
tute others for them. Above all, the monotheistic idea, even if associated with the
name of Zeus, tended to become an abstract
conception with little relation to the national god of Hellas, whom Phidias embodied in his Olympian statue.

The philosophic or theological conception
of a monotheistic deity does not, in fact,
seem to lend itself at any time to impressive artistic representation. We may
observe the same thing in Christian art,
in which representations of God the Father
are not very common nor, as a rule,
very expressive of the most vivid religious
ideals ; while Christ, usually not as God,

but as man or child, and the Virgin Mary are the constant themes of the most devout religious art, not to speak of the numerous saints who correspond more or less to the gods of a polytheistic system. Philosophical thought was antagonistic to anthropomorphism, which, as we have seen, was the most characteristic feature of popular religion in Greece, and which was essential to Greek religious art. As soon as the human form is a mere symbol, no longer regarded as the express image of the god and the embodiment of his individuality, it loses touch with reality. And this reality in the relation of the god to his image must be believed in by the people, and at least through the people by the artist, if religious art is to preserve its vitality.

CHAPTER III

CONDITIONS OF RELIGIOUS ART IN GREECE

THE Greeks possessed, as we have seen, to an exceptionally high degree the vivid anthropomorphic imagination necessary for the expression of their conception of the gods in their art ; we have also noticed the conditions which encouraged or restricted such representation, and the influences that affected its nature. Given the desire to represent the character and individuality of the gods in human form, the next question we have to consider is how far their art, and especially the art of sculpture, was capable of giving effect to this desire. The answer lies mainly in the history of Greek sculpture, which can only be touched on here in the barest outline. But,

48

at the outset, it is necessary to remove a misconception which is prevalent at the present day, and more especially in England, owing partly to the dominating influence of a great critic. Mr. Ruskin's *Aratra Pentelici* is full of the most admirable and suggestive appreciations of Greek sculpture in its more technical aspects ; but side by side with them are found passages such as the following : " There is no personal character in true Greek art ; abstract ideas of youth and age, strength and swiftness, virtue and vice—yes ; but there is no individuality." Or again : " The Greek, as such, never expresses personal character, while a Florentine holds it to be the ultimate condition of beauty." If this criticism were just, it would follow that any study of the relation of religion to art in Greece would lose most if not all of its interest. But anyone who is acquainted with the present state of our knowledge of Greek sculpture will not so much feel called upon to refute such statements as to explain how so strange a misconception could have arisen. Nor is the explanation very far to seek. Mr. Ruskin was writing for a generation not yet penetrated by the constructive criticism of recent investigation. Its conception of " the antique " in art was based mainly on the mass of mechanical and academic copies or imitations, of Græco-Roman date, with which our museums are filled, and on the influence of such sculpture to be seen in the work of Flaxman or Thorwaldsen. It had, indeed, learnt from the Elgin marbles that the Greek sculptors in the fifth century possessed a nobility in their conception of the human form, a mastery in the treatment of the nude and of drapery, and a skill in marble technique of which only a faint reflection can be traced in the later Græco-Roman tradition ; but the great statues in which the sculptors of the fifth century embodied their ideals of the gods were either entirely lost or pre served only in inadequate copies ; and it is only in recent years that the discovery of originals or the identification of trustworthy copies has enabled us to appreciate the intensity of expression and of inner life which distinguished the work of the great sculptors of the fourth century, such as Scopas, Praxiteles, and Lysippus. Still, if Mr. Ruskin had, like Brunn in his *Götter-idealen*, selected heads like those of the Demeter of Cnidus or the Hera Farnese to illustrate his theme, instead of a series of heads on coins magnified to many times the size for which they were designed, he could hardly have written the passages just quoted. But the second of those passages itself supplies us with another clue. In this estimate of Greek sculpture there is throughout implied a comparison with Christian, and above all with Florentine art, and its desire to

"... bring the invisible full into play ;
Let the visible go to the dogs ; what matters?"

It is evident that the expression of the invisible, of character and individuality, will be more striking and obvious in an art which lets them " shine through the flesh they fray " than in the case of the Greek sculptors whose respect and even passionate admiration for the human body would not allow them thus to transfigure it, at least in their statues of the gods, and led them to seek for subtler methods of expression by means of the flesh and in harmony with its nature. Their expression of character and emotion is rendered in terms of a beautiful and healthy body. How this end was attained we must consider later on ; but there is yet another current prejudice in favour of this exaggeration of individuality which has its influence especially upon modern artists. It is sometimes said nowadays that a departure from the individual model is an attempt to " improve upon nature," and is therefore an artistic mistake. Now the Greek sculptor, as a rule, did not work from an individual model at all. He trusted partly, especially in earlier times, to the tradition which familiarised him with a few fixed types, on which he made variations, partly to his observation and memory trained for generations, and daily supplied with new material in the gymnasium where nude youths and men were constantly exercising, or in the market-place where he met his fellow-citizens. To see before him, whether draped or nude, the figures he wanted for his art, he had no need to pose a model in a studio ; his models were at all times around him in his daily life. The result was that when he wished to represent a youth or a maiden, or even to make a portrait of a statesman, he tended to reproduce the type with certain personal modifications rather than to produce a portrait in the modern sense. But when he came to making statues of the gods, his freedom of hand was of incalculable service to him in giving a bodily form to his imagination ; it enabled him to create after nature, without being dependent on an individual model or having to fall back upon such vague and generalised forms as are sometimes associated with an academic or classical art ; for it was his own trained observation and memory that he called into play, not a mere mechanical system he had learnt from his predecessors. In the more individualistic art of the fourth century, as we shall see, it is probable that the personal model was of more importance, especially in female statues ; but even then it was still modified by the tradition and style which makes a harmonious whole, not only of each Greek statue, but of the development of Hellenic sculpture generally. In typical examples of the sculpture of the fourth century we find not only this harmony and restraint, and the beauty of bodily form in figure as well as in features which is generally recognised as characteristic of Greek art, but also an expression of character and individuality, of mood and temperament, of pathos and passion, which is none the less intense and real because it is expressed by means of the perfection of physical form, not as wasting or deforming it.

It may be asked how the invisible, mental, or spiritual qualities can be portrayed in visible form, especially if that visible form be not overmuch distorted or modified, and in a more general way, how the expression of a statue, and the impression it produces, can be analysed or discussed. For examples of the way this can be done, the reader may be referred once more to Brunn's *Götteridealen*, a study of a few selected representations of Greek gods in which the character of each is brought out by a subtle and discriminating analysis of the visible forms. Here it may suffice to quote Brunn's own words from the Introduction to that work : " The spiritual effect produced on us by a work of sculpture cannot be comprehended as a moral or a metaphysical peculiarity,

completely independent of corporeal phe-
nomena ; it can become intelligible to us
only by means of tangible sculptural forms,
as the exponents of spiritual expression."
And again : " The spiritual understanding of
ideal artistic creations can only be attained
on the basis of a thorough analysis of their
forms " ; hence in such a study we have
to do with " no subjective fancies, but an
investigation of objective artistic principles,
according to the method of scientific work."

There are various ways in which spiritual
qualities, mood, and character may be given
material expression in harmony with the
bodily forms, not in combat with the flesh.
There are, for instance, certain bodily
peculiarities that usually accompany, and
therefore suggest by association, various
temperaments or mental qualities ; and,
moreover, the actual effect upon the features
and bearing of certain emotions or moods
often leaves permanent traces, from which
a habitual or repeated tendency to such

emotions or moods can be inferred. That certain types of face and certain expressions are usually associated with certain spiritual or mental qualities will hardly be denied ; and here the method of the Greek artist, in observing and working from memory rather than from a posed model, gave him a great advantage in variety and freedom in the expression of character no less than in the rendering of bodily form. If he realised clearly the individuality of his gods, his skill and mastery over his material and his store of observation gave him a facility in giving this individuality a visible form which may not be so obvious at first sight as the individuality of a Florentine or of a modern head, but which is none the less there for those who have eyes to see it, and who can accustom themselves to the subtle atmosphere of ancient art, and to the moderation and restraint which are seldom, if ever, violated in its most characteristic productions.

CHAPTER IV

ANTHROPOMORPHISM

WE have already noticed the religious conceptions and impulses which led to the substitution of images in human shape for the rude stocks and stones of primitive worship. The beginning of the change seems to have taken place at an early stage in the development of Greek art. In pre-Hellenic times we find representation of gods and goddesses in human form upon gems and other small works of art, and also in statuettes that were either objects of worship or dedicated in shrines ; but we have at present no evidence as to whether monumental images of the gods were made in human form, though some objects of worship, such as the double-axe, were certainly set up in regular shrines. We know too little about the religious beliefs and customs of this prehistoric age to be able to judge whether such objects were regarded merely as symbols of the deity or as having immanent in them some divine or superhuman power ; but survivals, especially of an early tree and pillar cult, are probably to be traced in historic Greece, and even to the present day.

The Homeric poems, on the other hand, supply us with little or no evidence as to the existence of any sculptural representation of the gods. Although temples are frequently mentioned, we are not informed that any of them contained a sacred image, with the apparent exception of the temple of Athena at Troy. There we are told that the Trojan matrons, in a time of stress, brought a robe to offer to the goddess, and that the priestess Theano placed it " upon the knees of beauteous-haired Athene." Unless, as is possible, this is a purely metaphorical expression, it would seem to imply

a seated statue ; but it is to be noted that
the Palladium of Troy, the sacred image
of Athena which was stolen by Ulysses and
Diomed, and which was preserved, according
to conflicting traditions, in one or another
shrine in later Greece, was a standing statue
of a primitive type. The inconsistency is
not of great importance, except as showing
that the supposed mention of the statue of
Athena in the Iliad had little, if any, influence on later tradition ; and in any case
it is isolated, and does not refer to a Greek,
but a foreign temple. On the other hand,
we find frequent mention in later writers of
primitive statues of the gods which were
said to have been set up or dedicated by
various persons in the heroic age. An example is offered by the Trojan Palladium
already mentioned ; another was the statue
of Artemis carried off from Tauris by
Iphigenia and Orestes ; rival claimants to
this identification existed at Sparta and at
Brauron in Attica. The legends of dedica-

tion are of no historic value ; the story of the Palladium itself was unknown to Homer, though it occurred in later epics. All that can be asserted of such images is that they were of unknown antiquity, and that local patriotism claimed for them a heroic origin. Much the same may be said of Dædalus. It need not be discussed here whether an actual artist of this name ever existed. The information we have as to Dædalus is of two kinds ; on the one hand, we find tales of a mythical craftsman and magician, to whose invention many of the most typical improvements in early Greek sculpture are attributed ; on the other hand, we have records of many statues of the gods, extant in historical times in various shrines of Greece, which were attributed to him. Such attributions are not really of greater historical value than the traditions of dedication in the heroic age which we find elsewhere. The name of Dædalus having once become famous in this connection, it was natural that many statues of primitive style and unrecorded origin should be attributed to him. More importance may be attached to the fact that the sculptors who actually made some of the early statues of the gods in Athens and in the Peloponnesus are described as the pupils or by some as the sons or companions of Dædalus. In this way his name is associated with some of the early schools that had the greatest influence in Greece, especially on the representation of the gods in sculpture. There are other traditions of early schools of sculptors, the marble workers of Chios, the bronze founders of Samos, who devoted themselves mainly to making statues of the gods, some of which survived throughout historical times. When we turn from tradition and consider the early examples of statues of gods that may still be seen or are recorded by extant copies, we find that these fall into two classes. On the one hand, there are more or less exact repetitions of the primitive stock or stone, the cylindrical tree-trunk or the rectangular block cut from the quarry, with the rudest indication of head and arms and feet, deviating as little as possible from the original shape of the block. When images of this sort were, as was often the case, of wood, they have, of course, disappeared ; but we can sometimes recognise copies of them upon reliefs or in stone. On the other hand, we find another class of images which approximate more to the attainments of Dædalus as described by rationalising writers of later date. These images are completely in human form, and, if male, are usually nude. They have their legs separated in a short stride, the left foot being usually advanced ; their arms are either set close to their sides, or one or both of them is raised from the elbow ; their whole shape suggests a rigid system of proportions and a more or less conventionalised form. These images have no resemblance to the modifications of the primitive stocks and stones, and could not well be directly derived from them; they are found in great numbers upon many sites of early sanctity in Greece itself and in Greek settlements around the Levant, notably in Cyprus, Rhodes, and Naucratis in Egypt. Sometimes they seem to represent the god, sometimes the dedicator; but all alike show the attempt of the early Greek craftsman to imitate the products of more advanced and finished art which he saw around him. Many of them are derived from Egyptian types; others show the influence of Mesopotamian art, or of the hybrid craftsmanship of Phœnicia. The borrowing or imitation of such foreign types may at first sight appear to show even less promise of artistic progress than variations on the old native images; but it is not in its origins, but in its development and perfection that the chief excellence of Greek art is to be found.

The types borrowed by sculpture from

foreign art are almost exclusively of human form. The monstrous mixed forms in which the deities of Egypt or Mesopotamia often found the expression of their super-human and mysterious powers do not seem to have appealed to the imagination of the Greeks. Such mixed forms were, indeed, frequently borrowed by early decorative art, and on " Orientalising " vases we constantly find human-headed and bird-headed quad-rupeds, usually winged, and human-headed birds. The delight in winged figures gener-ally, which was mainly decorative in early times, also finds its origin in Oriental woven stuffs. Greek sculpture adopted and trans-lated into stone or bronze some of these mixed types—notably the human-headed bird and the human-headed winged lion ; these it identified as the Siren and the Sphinx of Greek myth, and associated them with the mysteries of the tomb. To some other forms, that of the Centaur and the Satyr and the Triton, it also gave considerable scope. But all these, if not human, are hardly to be regarded as divine ; they are mostly noxious, and, even if benignant, do not attain the rank of gods. Perhaps a nearer approach to divine character is to be found in the river-gods, who are often represented as bulls with human heads or as human with bull's horns ; but here, too, we have only to deal with minor deities. No sculptor represented Dionysus in this way, even though he was called " bull-shaped " by poets ; nor is the horse-god Posidon even represented as a Centaur. The horse-headed Demeter of Phigalia remains the strange and solitary exception, however we may explain her existence.

The process by which the early human types were gradually improved and made more life-like, by a continuous struggle with technical difficulties, by constant and direct observation of nature, and by the building up of an artistic tradition in different schools and families, is a question that concerns the history of art rather than our present study. But it is impossible to distinguish rigidly between the two, because these types, whether of the nude standing male figure, of the draped female, or of the seated figure, are all of them used alike to represent human and divine personages; and, apart from inscriptions of dedication or conditions of discovery or distinctive attributes, it would often be impossible to tell whether any particular statue was meant to represent, for example, the image of a god or a conventional portrait of a man. These nude male statues, commonly known by the name of " Apollo," were certainly, some of them, made to commemorate athletes, whose images were set up either in the place where they won their victories or in their native town ; others were placed over graves as memorials of the dead ; and even in a sacred precinct it is sometimes uncertain whether the god himself is represented or the worshipper who dedicates this record of his devotion.

At this early period, therefore, Mr. Ruskin's strictures as to the impossibility of distinguishing the individuality of the different gods must be admitted, and even supplemented by an admission of the impossibility of distinguishing gods and goddesses from human beings. The explanation is obvious enough. During this age of early progress the constant aim of the sculptor is to attain to complete mastery over the material and to perfection of bodily form. In religious art, what corresponds to this is the struggle towards anthropomorphism—first to represent the gods in human form, and then to make that form the most perfect that human art can devise. During this stage of artistic and religious development the type and the ideal cannot be distinguished. It was only when a type or a varying series of types had been brought to perfection in the fifth century, so as to satisfy the demand for a harmonious system of bodily proportions, for beauty of outline and dignity of countenance, that these types could be used as a means of expression for the religious ideals of the nation. In developing the type the accidental has to be discarded, and with it much of the feeling of individuality ; works of early archaic art, for all their defects, often show more sign of individual character than the more perfect works of the earlier part of the fifth century. The attainment of the type is followed by an infusion of character and individuality, drawn from the artist's trained memory and observation with clear artistic intention, not from the mere caprice of an accidental recollection or a casual peculiarity of a model. The character and individuality thus expressed must be considered in subsequent chapters ; it is only necessary here to distinguish it from the suggestion of an individual, almost of a caricature, which we find sometimes in archaic art, and which is certainly to be seen occasionally in works of Florentine sculpture. During the period of the rise of Greek sculpture the various schools were advancing each in its own way towards what has been called naturalism in art, as opposed to realism on the one side and idealism on the other. That is to say, they were striving by constant study of the athletic form, of proportions and muscles, of drapery and hair, to attain to a series of types both in harmony with themselves and in accordance with nature ; and they were too much absorbed in this attempt to go far beyond their predecessors in rendering the character of the gods according to the form consecrated by tradition. Even in the expression of the face the same process is to be traced. In early works we find sometimes no expression at all, or an apparent stolidity which is really the absence of expression ; in the archaic smile we see an attempt to enliven the face, and possibly also, as we have noticed, to express and even to induce the benignity of the deity. But this attempt, made with inadequate artistic resources, tends to result in a mere grimace ; and as we approach the transitional age before the greatest period of sculpture, we often find a reaction against any such exaggeration of expression in a severity and dignity that may have a certain grace of their own, but that are in some sense a retrograde movement so far as the expression of character is concerned.

It follows that the statues of the gods dating from this early period, however interesting they might be for the history of sculpture, would not, even if we possessed many more of them than we do possess, throw very much light upon the development of the ideas of the Greeks concerning their deities. They would probably conform to a limited number of clearly defined types. The most familiar of all, the standing nude male figure, would, if beardless, usually represent Apollo, with a bow or a branch of bay, or sometimes other attributes. A similar type, bearded, would stand for Zeus or Posidon or Hermes, if provided with thunderbolt or eagle, with trident or fish, or with a caduceus. Similar figures might also be draped, and still represent gods ; or, if female, would serve for Hera, Artemis, Aphrodite, and sometimes for Athena, if she was represented without her arms and ægis. Then, too, there was the seated type, usually enveloped in full drapery, which might readily be adapted to a statue of any of the chief gods. In all of these there is no question of distinguishing the gods from one another in character and individuality ; apart from attributes, there is hardly any attempt to distinguish gods from men.

Perhaps the earliest class of statues in which we find any attempt to give artistic expression to superhuman power is that in which we see the god in vigorous action, often striking with his characteristic weapon : Zeus with his thunderbolt in his raised right hand, Posidon with his trident, or Athena advancing rapidly with brandished spear and shield advanced. But even these figures, apart from their divine attributes, show no essential distinction from human combatants. It is a significant fact that it is still a matter of dispute* whether one of the most famous statues of the early fifth century, " the Choiseul-Gouffier Apollo," represents a god or an athlete. This is neither because the Greeks at this time idealised their athletes nor because they humanised their gods, but because they typified them both ; that is to say, they represented them by a type which was the most perfect rendering within their power either of man or of an anthropomorphic deity. Here we have the material form provided by means of which the ideals of the succeeding period were to find their artistic expression—such a typical or normal human form is, in fact, the logical expression

* Even if this dispute be regarded as now settled by weight of evidence, the fact that such a dispute is possible retains its significance.

of anthropomorphism in its most literal sense—the making of gods after man's image. But those who believed rather that man was made after God's image would look to find in the prototype something more and higher than can be seen in its earthly copy. This notion, even if not formulated by philosophy until a later age, certainly underlies the idealistic art of the fifth century.

CHAPTER V

IDEALISM

THE age which followed the great Persian Wars was the time of the highest political, literary, and intellectual development in Greece. Nor was it unfavourable to strength and depth of religious feeling among the people. If the more thoughtful among them were inclined to doubt whether some of the stories told about the gods were either probable or edifying, these were the very men who, on the other hand, were most capable of appreciating the higher and nobler conceptions of the gods which we find in contemporary poets. And the great delivery from the Persians not only gave the Greeks a confidence in themselves which justly increased their national pride and thereby strengthened their national ideals, but it also gave occasion to a confidence in the gods and a gratitude to them which found expression in numerous buildings and offerings. All this religious activity could not fail to have considerable influence upon the common people ; and in some cases, as at Athens, there was the necessity of replacing the temples and statues that had been destroyed or carried off by the Persian invader. At the time when a demand occurred for new statues of the gods, the rapid progress of the art of sculpture made it inevitable that these new statues should not be mere reproductions or reminiscences of the ones they replaced, but fresh and original conceptions, worthy of the increased skill of the artist and of the nobler ideals of the people. And by one of those coincidences which we meet so often both in the history of art and in that of literature, just at the time when the material conditions, the spirit of the people, and the rapid advance of art gave the utmost scope for artistic creation, there arose the man of transcendent genius to give full expression to the religious and artistic aspirations of the time. The age of Pericles was also the age of Phidias. It is true that there was an interval between the defeat of the Persians and the period of highest attainment in Greece ; and during this interval many temples were built or rebuilt, and many statues were set up as objects of worship or as dedications to the gods. Some of these may have anticipated to a certain extent the work of Phidias ; several of them were of colossal size, like his chief masterpieces, and thus, even from the technical point of view, may have prepared the way before him ; one, the Apollo by Calamis at Apollonia, was about forty-five feet high, and so actually rivalled the Zeus and Athena of Phidias in size. But of these statues we know little or nothing. As to the two most famous works of Phidias himself, the Athena Parthenos within the Parthenon at Athens

and the Zeus at Olympia, we are better informed, so far as elaborate descriptions and
the somewhat rhetorical appreciations of
later writers are concerned ; and we possess
some extant copies which tell us something
of their pose and attributes. But any notion
we may form as to their true artistic and
religious character must be mainly dependent upon our imagination ; and even for
their relation to the religious ideals of the
people we are dependent for the most part
upon indirect evidence. Though the art of
sculpture was so closely bound up with the
life of the people in Greece, we find very
few references to its greatest works ; it is
evident that the Athenians, for example,
took the greatest pride in the buildings that
adorned their Acropolis and in the sculp-
tures they contained ; yet when Pericles, as
reported by Thucydides, speaks of the
statue of the Athena Parthenos, it is only
to reckon the gold of her drapery as part of
the possible resources of the state.   We

know that in the eyes of Pericles and of his hearers the preciousness of the material was only an incident in the artistic character of the work ; but what is felt most deeply is often the least spoken about. Later descriptions, such as that of Pausanias, lay emphasis on the details and accessories of the statue, the ornamentation of helmet and shield and sandals ; they lay themselves open to the stricture of Lucian on " such as can neither see nor praise the whole beauty of the Olympian Zeus, great and noble as it is, nor describe it to others that do not know it, but admire the accurate work and fine polish of his footstool and the good proportions of the basis, enumerating all such details with the utmost care." At the same time even such information as they give us is welcome, since it aids our imagination to reconstruct the appearance of the whole. These great chryselephantine statues were placed within the cella of a temple, lighted only through the door and

by some infiltration through the marble
roof, and their effect was calculated for
these conditions. The rich tone and subtle
reflections of the ivory and the gold, mingled
with coloured inlays of enamel or precious
stones, and tempered and harmonised by a
" dim religious light," must have been most
impressive ; and the grandeur of the figures
was enhanced by their colossal size. But
in all this we are still dealing only with conditions and accessories, not with the art
itself and the religious ideals which it expressed. These are perhaps easier for us to
appreciate in the case of the Zeus than of
the Athena, though we are better provided
with copies of the latter. We are accus-
tomed in our own religious art to the attempt to express divinity in the form of a
mature man of unspeakable majesty and
benignity. To the Greeks, indeed, the
human figure of Zeus was not merely an
incarnation, but the actual form of the god
himself ; the god was not thought of as

having taken upon himself the sorrows and the weaknesses of our mortal nature, but as sharing only its ideal perfection. Yet that the effect was not altogether dissimilar is shown by such a passage as that we find in Dion Chrysostom : " A man whose soul is utterly immersed in toil, who has suffered many disasters and sorrows, and cannot even enjoy sweet sleep, even such an one, I think, if he stood face to face with this statue, would forget all the dangers and difficulties of this mortal life : such the vision you, Phidias, have invented and devised, a sight ' to lull all pain and anger, and bring forgetfulness of every sorrow.' "

The same writer elsewhere puts into the mouth of Phidias an explanation of how he had attempted to embody in his statue the current conception of the god, and even the epithets that belonged to his worship. " My Zeus," says the sculptor, " is peaceful and altogether gentle, as the guardian of a Hellas free from factions and of one mind

with itself. Him, taking counsel with my
art, and with the wise and noble Elean state,
I set up in his temple, mild and majestic in
a form free from all sorrow, as the giver of
life and livelihood and all good things, the
common father of men, their saviour and
their guardian, so far as it is possible for a
mortal man to conceive and to copy his
divine and inexpressible nature. And consider whether you will not find the image
according with all the epithets of the god ;
Zeus alone is called the father of gods and
their only king, and also god of the city and
of friendship and society, and of suppliants
too and strangers, the giver of harvest, and
by innumerable other titles. And for one
whose aim it was to display all these qualities without speaking, is not my art successful ? The strength of the form and its
imposing proportions show the power to
rule and the king ; the gentle and amiable
character shows the father and his care ;
the majesty and severity show the god of

the city and of law ; and of the kinship of
men and gods the similarity of their shape
serves as a symbol. His protective friendship of suppliants and strangers and fugitives
and such like is seen in his kindliness and his
evident gentleness and goodness. And an
image of the giver of possessions and harvest
is seen in the simplicity and magnanimity
displayed in his form ; he seems just like
one who would give and be generous of
good things. All this, in short, I imitated as
far as possible, being unable to express it in
speech." This description is, of course, the
work of a late and rhetorical author, but it
is the work of a man who was familiar with
these great statues that are now lost to
us, and was capable of appreciating them.
His criticism may not be so thorough and
subtle as the analysis of the Greek type of
Zeus made by Brunn in his *Götteridealen ;*
but it is based on similar principles, the
observation of the physical type and the
spiritual expression which serves best to

embody the majesty and benignity of the god. After all, we come back perhaps to the saying of Phidias himself, and his quotation from Homer; here, too, it is the brow of the god that is emphasised, and the nod that shook Olympus while it granted a prayer. It is in such effects rather than in any detailed description that it is possible to realise the nature of a great work of art.

What success in the attainment of its aim was here reached by the art of the sculptor may perhaps best be estimated from the often quoted sentence of Quintilian, perhaps the noblest praise ever accorded to an artist by a critic: " The beauty of the statue even made some addition to the received religion; the majesty of the work was equal to the god." We might indeed, without irreverence, impute to Phidias the words uttered in a very different sense by one who later gave a new and higher interpretation to a formula of " the received religion " in

Greece : " Whom therefore ye ignorantly worship, Him declare I unto you."

The other great Phidian ideal, that of Athena, was represented by several statues, both in Athens and in other cities. As to these we have a certain amount of information, and even a certain number of copies, which show us the pose and the accessories of the various statues ; some of the better ones even suffice to give us some notion of the beauty of their original. We have also descriptions by ancient writers, which tell us, as in the case of the Olympian Zeus, much about the decoration of the statue ; but we have not in this case any appreciations of the effect upon those who saw it. The ideal of Athena is in some ways more difficult for us to comprehend than that of Zeus, partly because it is less universally human, and more peculiarly characteristic of Greece and even of Athens. The notion of the mother goddess is common to most religions ; that of the " queen and huntress,

chaste and fair " is at least familiar to us
in literature, and readily commends itself
to the imagination. But Athena, though
she has something of both these characters,
has a nature different from both. It is
impossible to derive her varied mythological
functions from any one origin ; but here it
is not the origin of her worship that concerns us, rather its meaning and influence as
these affected the people of her chosen city.
Just as Zeus was the ideal of all that was
best in the Hellenic conception of manhood
and the god of a united Hellas, so Athena
is especially the goddess of Athens, the
giver and fosterer of all those qualities that
made the Athenians what they were, the
creatress of that ideal city sketched in the
wonderful speeches of Pericles. Her gifts
are the arts of war and peace, and all artistic
and intellectual activity, as well as the olive
and other characteristic products of Attic
soil, and the clear and luminous air and
stimulating climate which Attic writers are

never tired of extolling, and of associating
with the peculiar genius of the Athenian
race. One can imagine how Dion Chrysostom
might have recognised the expression of
these various qualities in the broad and
majestic, yet keenly intellectual brow, in
the wide and clear eyes, and in other
features ; but the extant copies of the
Athena Parthenos cannot do more than
assist our imagination in realising how the
sculptor represented the goddess of Athens.
Here, too, as in the case of the Zeus, it is
difficult for us to avoid the error of regarding
the statue as a mere philosophical abstraction, an impersonation of the qualities it
represents. Athena in later art, as set up in
libraries and museums, was doubtless such
an impersonation, just as she is in modern
art unreal and comparatively uninteresting.
But the Athenian believed intensely in the
existence of his goddess. He believed that
the ceremonies connected with her ancient
image were necessary to the continuance of

her favour to her city and people, and that the new temples and statues set up in her honour would still further delight her and ensure her protection and her abode among her grateful worshippers. The statue by Phidias within the Parthenon offered not merely that form in which she would choose to appear if she showed herself to mortal eyes, but actually showed her form as she had revealed it to the sculptor. To look upon such an image helped the worshipper as much as—perhaps more than—any service or ritual to bring himself into communion with the goddess, and to fit himself, as a citizen of her chosen city, to carry out her will in contributing his best efforts to its supremacy in politics, in literature, and in art. If a work of art could have this actual influence upon religious emotion, and through it upon practical life, it may be said to have attained the utmost that any human effort can achieve in the service of God.

IDEALISM

The religious influence of art in the fifth century is, as we have seen, closely associated with the state ; the Athena Parthenos and the Olympian Zeus appealed to their worshippers as citizens of Athens and as members of the privileged Hellenic race. It would be easy to trace a similar character in almost all the great statues of gods that are recorded as belonging to this period. Thus the Dionysus of Alcamenes is not the dreamy god of wine and pleasure that we find at a later age, but an august figure, bearded and enthroned, the giver of the riches of the earth and the wine, the god in whose honour all the great Dionysian festivals were held ; the same sculptor's Hermes is the guardian of ways and gates, the giver of increase to flocks, not the youthful and athletic messenger of the gods. Hephæstus, too, especially when associated with Athena, is the patron and teacher of all handicrafts, himself the ideal artisan, practical and genial, but with none of his

godhead lost in a too human individuality ;
even his lameness—characteristic of the
smith in all folk-lore—is lightly indicated,
not dwelt on as an interesting motive.
Various statues of particular gods may, of
course, emphasise one side or another of
their functions. Athena may be worshipped
and represented as goddess of Victory or of
Health ; but here, too, it is usually some
recognised state cult that underlies the
representation. Outside Athens we find
the same conditions. To take only one instance, the colossal gold and ivory Hera of
Argos, made by the chief Argive master
Polyclitus, is the great goddess of the city,
just as Athena is of Athens. She was
represented as the bride of Zeus, who
annually renewed her maidenhood at the
great Argive festival of the divine marriage ;
and we cannot doubt that Polyclitus expressed in this statue, which was hardly less
famous than the masterpieces of Phidias, all
the essential features of the great religious

ideals that underlay this primitive rite. His Hera had neither the warlike nor the intellectual and spiritual characteristics of the Attic Athena ; but she was the goddess of womanly grace and beauty in the bride, and embodied that perfection of physical form which Argive art sought also in its athletic figures, and which was in a sense a part of the religion that found expression in the great athletic games. Some gods—Apollo, for example—seem in fifth-century statues to have a more individual character. Just as in earlier times the name Apollo serves to cover a multitude of statues of which some may be meant to represent individual men, so even in the age of Phidias we sometimes meet with a figure of athletic type or of youthful beauty as to which it is possible to doubt whether it is an Apollo ; this may be partly the result of the great popularity of the type in all ages of Greek sculpture which led to its more rapid development and earlier individualisation. But the

Apollo of this period is never the mere
dreamy youth of later time ; it has been
well said that he is the god who, in the
mythical athletic contest, could surpass
Hermes in the foot-race and Ares in boxing ;
the embodiment of all-round physical and
intellectual excellence, the combination of
music and gymnastic, which again brings
us back to a national Hellenic ideal.
Throughout the representations of the gods
in the art of the fifth century we find the
same essential character. They embody in
themselves the expression, by means of
the most perfect physical forms, of the
qualities attributed to the god himself, or
given by him to his worshippers. They are
no impersonal abstraction of these qualities,
but are real and living beings, in whom
these qualities exist to a degree impossible
for a mere mortal. But, on the other hand,
they have nothing of the passions and emotions, the weaknesses and imperfections of
mortal nature. In this they are inconsis-

tent, perhaps, with that Homeric presentment of the gods which the greatest artists
consciously set before themselves. But we
cannot wonder that an age of such clear and
lofty intellectual and moral perceptions
should have rejected what it felt to be unworthy in the current notions of the gods, and
should have selected only what it felt to be
truly divine. Art did not, however, remain
very long upon its highest level of religious
feeling ; but in Greece, by a fortunate coin-
cidence, the age of the greatest religious
ideals was also that of the highest perfection
of physical type in art as well as of technical
skill in execution. We do not therefore find
in this age that the sculptor lacks the power
to express his ideas, or that his ideas are too
strong for the forms in which they are expressed ; there is rather that perfect harmony between the two that, here as elsewhere, is characteristic of Hellenic art.

CHAPTER VI

INDIVIDUALISM

THE great religious ideals of the fifth century were, as we have seen, closely bound up with the subordination of the individual to the State ; and their expression in sculpture was also due in almost every case to the employment of the artist by the community. In the fourth century, on the other hand, we find on every side a stronger assertion of individuality. It was a commonplace among Attic orators in the fourth century to contrast the private luxury and ostentation of their own day with the simplicity of life among the great men of the earlier age, whose houses could not be distinguished from those of the common people, though their public buildings and the temples they raised to the gods were of unparalleled splendour. In religion, and above all in religious art, we find something of the same tendency. There are few if any records of the dedication during the fourth century of those great statues of the chief gods which were looked back to by all subsequent generations as the embodiment of a national ideal. But there were, perhaps, more statues of the gods made in the fourth century which were the objects not merely of artistic admiration, but of intense and sometimes morbid personal devotion. The mere list of the gods preferred for representation is an indication in itself; while in the fifth century, Zeus and Athena and Hera, the great gods of the State or of the Hellenic race, are the subjects of the most famous statues, in the fourth century it is rather Aphrodite and Dionysus and Asclepius, those whose gifts contribute to individual happiness or enjoyment, that offer most scope to the powers of the artist.

And the sculptors themselves, in the fourth century, show more individuality of style. In the latter part of the fifth century the genius of Phidias had so dominated religious art that the works of his successors, men like Alcamenes and Agoracritus, could hardly be distinguished from his. But the great sculptors of the fourth century, Scopas and Praxiteles and Lysippus, not to mention others of less note, devoted themselves not so much to the expression through perfect physical form of great religious ideals, but to a realisation of the character and, so to speak, the personality of the gods whom they portrayed. And they did this by the same means by which they expressed in their art the characters and passions of heroes or of men, thereby removing the gods from the sphere of passionless benignity and power which is assigned to them by the art of the fifth century. Such a treatment evidently gave more scope for variety in the styles of the

sculptors ; and although we can sometimes
trace the influence of one upon another, yet
each clearly shows his own characteristics.
We are expressly told of Praxiteles that he
showed the most admirable skill in infusing
into his marble works the passions and
emotions of the soul ; and the extant remains of the statues made by Scopas and
Lysippus show that they also, each in his
own way, attained the same results.

If the sculpture of the fifth century was
ethical, expressing noble ideals of character
whether in gods or men, that of the fourth
century may be called psychological. It is
not content with character ; it expresses also
mood and even passion, and thereby gives
more prominence to individuality. At first
sight it is not easy to realise how this
change came to affect the representations of
the gods. The gods of Homer are, indeed,
full of individual character; but we have seen
how in the fifth century, though the greatest
sculptors declared it was the gods of Homer

that they represented, these representations were idealised and raised above those human touches in which the individuality is most conspicuous. There was, in the Homeric hymns and in the lyric poets, a delight in details of incident and in personal peculiarities and even in romantic tales about the gods ; and in the fourth century, when the high idealisation of the preceding age is no longer so strong in its influence, we find a similar tendency in art as well. While the great statues of the gods in the fifth century are almost all represented as either enthroned or standing, not employed in any particular action or function, the most characteristic examples of the statues of gods made in the fourth century have almost all some definite motive. We may take as an example what was perhaps the most famous statue of antiquity, the Aphrodite by Praxiteles at Cnidus. The goddess is represented as nude ; and it is often said that goddesses would not have been so represented in the fifth century. It is true that full drapery seems more consistent with the dignified and august figures of Phidian art. But if the religious type had required that Phidias should make a nude goddess, we may be sure he would have made her naked and unashamed, with no more self-consciousness than a nude Apollo ; above all, he would not have thought it necessary to provide a motive for her nudity. With Praxiteles it is otherwise. He represents the goddess as preparing for the bath, and just letting her last garment slip from her hand on to a vase that stands beside her ; and, in addition to this provision of a motive —an excuse, one might almost say—for representing her without her clothes, he hints, from the instinctive gesture of her other hand which she holds before her body, at a half-conscious shrinking from exposure, a feeling of modesty which, however suitable to a woman, is by no means consistent with a high ideal of the goddess. The

face and figure are of extraordinary physical
beauty of type, of a breadth and nobility
which contrast with the smaller, prettier,
and less dignified forms of later art ; the
gesture, too, has not the conscious coquetry
which we see in such a work as the Venus de'
Medici. But, on the other hand, we must
recognise that the statue represents the
goddess under a human rather than a divine
aspect, that even her mood and feeling of
timidity are portrayed in a manner which,
however charming in itself, is totally incon-
sistent with her worship as a great goddess.
We are not surprised to hear that this statue
inspired a personal passion ; she is the
goddess of love, and is represented as not
beyond the reach of human attraction ;
but she is brought down to the level of
mortals, rather than capable of raising
mortals to a higher sphere by her contemplation. It is the same, though perhaps to
a less degree, with other statues of the gods
made in the fourth century. The motives

with which the later Greeks went to visit the great statues of the Phidian age were, as we have seen, to a great extent religious, and their contemplation was regarded to some extent as a service ; here we have " idolatry " in its highest form. But those who went to see the Aphrodite of Cnidus went chiefly to enjoy the beauty of the statue ; and although this may be the best thing from the artistic point of view, it certainly has not the same religious import.

There is another element in the individuality of fourth-century statues which may appeal to modern artists, and which certainly did appeal—in an inverted manner —to early Christian writers of invectives against pagan idolatry. It was said that Phryne had posed as a model for the Cnidian Aphrodite of Praxiteles ; and the character of the goddess was inferred from that of her votary. It is clear that a Greek artist could not have, in the case of a nude female statue, the same choice of types constantly present to his observation and his memory as he had in the case of male statues ; and the individuality of the model, however beautiful, would thus tend to assert itself against the type. Thus personality and individual character, " the ultimate condition of beauty," to use Mr. Ruskin's words, in modern as in Tuscan art, comes much nearer to expression in the fourth century than in the fifth. But a study of such a statue as the Cnidian Aphrodite shows us nevertheless that in the beauty of the type and the avoidance of the accidental, the art of Praxiteles was as far removed from realism as it was from the vague generalisation of Græco-Roman and modern pseudo-classical art. It is full of life and individuality, but it is the individuality of a character realised within his mind by the artist, not merely copied from the human model he set before him.

Another method by which the motive becomes prominent in the art of the fourth century is to be seen in the interpretation of mythological conceptions. These are realised and embodied in statues; but the statues offer a new, sometimes, it seems, almost an accidental and trifling version of a solemn religious conception; it appears as if the artist were playing with a mythological subject. Thus in the statue made by Praxiteles of Apollo Saurokto-nos, " the lizard-slayer," the god stands with an arrow in his hand, as if trying to catch with it a lizard who runs up a tree; it suggests a boyish game rather than the epithet of a god. Again, the worship of Artemis Brauronia at Athens was one of the oldest and most sacred cults in the city, and women at marriage and at other critical times of their life used to offer her their garments, thereby bringing themselves into close contact with the goddess and claiming her special protection, the garments being actually placed on the old image. If, as is probable, the Artemis of Gabii is a copy of the statue substituted by Praxiteles for this old image, we see there the goddess, as a graceful girlish figure, fastening a cloak upon her shoulder. This may be taken as symbolical of the earlier custom of placing the garments on the statue ; but we have evidence that the worshippers were not content with such a symbolic contact, but had the actual garments placed on the new statue as they had been on the old. Here we have probably a case of unsuccessful substitution ; the artistic representation did not suffice to replace the actual rite. But the representation itself is doubtless intended in a way which, however graceful, does not represent any deep religious feeling ; one feels that the artist found the subject a convenient one as an artistic motive, rather than that he had any deep religious idea to express.

We must not, however, go too far in denying religious ideals to the fourth century altogether. Some of the gods, who came very near to the life of man, but who were nevertheless worshipped with a real belief in their power and benevolence, found at this time their fullest expression in art. An example may be seen in the Demeter of Cnidus, the mother sorrowing for her daughter, whose suffering brings her into close sympathy with human weakness, and whose mysteries, perhaps more than any other Hellenic service, brought men and women into personal communion with the gods. We may take as another instance the head of Asclepius from Melos in the British Museum. Here, as Brunn has pointed out in his admirable analysis of its forms, we may recognise not so much the god as the half-human, half-divine physician, a genial and friendly spirit who persuades rather than commands. The expression is not only intellectual, but has also an infinite gentleness, as of one not himself unacquainted with mortal pain and sorrow ; and such a conception, as we know from Christian art, often appeals to those who find the majesty of Zeus too distant, the idea of his godhead too abstract. In such almost human ideals the individuality of the fourth century finds its full scope, as in other half-human creations of the artist's imagination. Apollo as the inspired musician or—if we accept the derivation of the Apollo Belvedere from a fourth-century original—as the disdainful archer, Hermes, the protector and playmate of his little brother Dionysus, and many other such representations of the gods in their personal moods and characteristic actions, seem in many ways less divine, less full of religious feeling than such an Asclepius ; if the great gods are brought too near to human passions and weaknesses, they cannot but lose much of their divinity.

One might easily multiply examples of similar motives in the statues of the gods made in the fourth century ; but we should find the same underlying principles in all cases. The gods are indeed more clearly realised as having personal character and individuality, and for this reason they may sometimes inspire keener personal feelings of worship or even of romantic devotion. But the older and higher conceptions of the gods, as an essential part of the State religion, and as embodying the ideals of the race or of the city, are no longer to be found, except in a somewhat lifeless continuance of the fifth-century tradition. The intensity of expression which we find in human heroes is, indeed, expressed also in such types as that of Apollo the musician or of Dionysus the god of inspired enthusiasm. But this tendency is not fully developed until a later age. The subtle distinctions of character between the different gods are, on the other hand, now most keenly observed and most skilfully rendered. But in spite of this, one does not feel that the artist has the same belief in the gods and in their power as we can see in the Phidian age. If his artistic attainment is possibly more skilful, the religious import of his work is certainly less.

CHAPTER VII

PERSONIFICATION, CONVENTION, AND SYMBOLISM

IN the Hellenistic age we find the Greek types of the gods adapting themselves to new conditions and new meanings. With the conquests of Alexander, Greek language and civilisation spread over the Eastern world; and with them went the artistic forms of the Greek pantheon, though often to be modified by local beliefs or influences. Similarly, when at a later time the Roman conquest of Greece spread Hellenic influence to the West, there also the types of the Greek deities came to be adopted or adapted to new mythological meanings. Greek art practically became cosmopolitan; its influence was broadened; but at the same time its essential nature, in its harmony with the imagination of the Hellenic race, was lost or obscured. It becomes more intelligible to us for this very reason, but at the same time less instructive in its relation to religious conceptions.

In the art of the Hellenistic and Græco-Roman age we find two main tendencies, the one towards academic generalisation, and the other towards excessive realism, often coupled with a theatrical or sensational treatment. This latter is the more interesting to us, partly because it is in itself more original, partly because it is more in accordance with modern artistic practice. The two tendencies are by no means rigidly distinguished ; for example, we often find a theatrical treatment combined with academic work ; and throughout are to be seen traces of eclecticism—that is to say, of the habit of imitating or reproducing, often in an unintelligent manner, the devices and even the style of earlier art. It does not follow that no great works of art were made in the Hellenistic age ; the fine traditions of the fifth and fourth centuries were not easily lost. But the inspiration of the subject, so far as it still exists, comes from new and different sources.

If we consider first the statues of the older gods of Greece, we often find in them the individualistic tendencies of the fourth century carried to a further pitch—sometimes to an extreme—in the sentimental or passionate works of the Hellenistic age ; there is often something affected or dramatic about them, as if they were not merely realised as expressing their individual character in their mood or action, but acting their part as the representative of such a character ; in fact, they tend to embody impersonations rather than to express personalities. One might almost repeat here much that has been said about the gods in the fourth century, but that there is often, in this case, a touch of exaggeration which is avoided by the finer artistic instinct and appreciation of harmony that mark the work of earlier sculptors ; and joined with this we often find a love of display and a seeking after effect which imply that the artist thinks more of his skill than of the idea he is striving to express.

We can trace in the Hellenistic age not only the traditions of earlier art, but the direct influence of the masters of the fourth century, the Praxitelean cult of beauty for its own sake, the passion and dramatic force of Scopas, and the preference for allegorical subjects and for statues of colossal size which we may see, as well as many higher qualities, in the art of Lysippus. We have already noticed how in the Apollo Belvedere there is an impression of theatrical posing which was probably either introduced by the copyist or at any rate much exaggerated by him in imitating an earlier type ; and how in the Venus de' Medici we find a crude insistence on a gesture of mock modesty which is a mere

travesty of the hint at half-conscious
shrinking from exposure which we see in
the Cnidian Aphrodite. Even in a statue
which, like the Aphrodite of Melos, shows
an endeavour to return to the nobler ideals
and more dignified and simple forms of
an earlier age, there is something artificial
and conventional about both figure and
drapery ; and one feels that the sculptor,
though both his aims and his attainments
are of the highest, is trying rather to reflect
the best influences of his predecessors than
to embody a present religious conception.

The influence upon art of religious personifications is perhaps stronger than any
other during this period. There had, indeed,
been such personifications at an earlier
time, such as the statue by Cephisodotus
of Peace nursing the infant Wealth. The
most interesting example of such personification may be seen in the figures of cities,
or, to speak more accurately, of the For-
tunes of cities, such as the Antioch of

Eutychides.   The influence of the city or
state upon religious art was conspicuous in
the fifth century ; but here we find the city
itself or its presiding genius represented in
a statue which seems at first sight a mere
allegory of its situation.   The way in which
the figure is seated, half turned on herself,
and with her feet resting upon the shoulder
of the river that swims below her, seems to
suggest an artificially invented symbolism ;
yet we are expressly told that this statue
received great veneration from the natives
of the district.   In the decay of the belief in
the gods, there seems to have been a craving
for nearer and more real objects of worship.

We can see the same tendency in a
more extreme form in the deification of
human beings.   Though some examples of
this occur earlier, especially in the case
of the heroes or founders of cities, these
are not placed on a level with the gods ;
but the worship of Alexander, and in imitation of him, of his successors, placed him

in a distinctly divine rank. It is difficult
to say how far this was due to non-Hellenic
influences. In the case of Alexander, with
his marvellous, almost superhuman achieve-
ments, and his final solution of the great
drama of the contest of East and West,
such idealisation is easy to understand ;
and we find not only that Alexander is
himself represented as a god, but that his
expression and cast of features come to
affect the sculpture of his age, even in the
representations of the gods themselves.
On coins, too, his head occurs ; an honour
that before his time was not given to mere
mortals. In other cases this worship of men
reached a pitch which was a matter of shame
to the later Greeks ; thus Demetrius Polior-
cetes, when he gave Athens back her freedom, was welcomed at the city with divine
honours. Even hymns were composed in
his honour, of which we find specimens
preserved.* After welcoming his advent

* Athen., VI, 63.

at the same time as that of Demeter, the poet addresses him thus:—" Other gods are either far away, or they have no ears, or they exist not, or have no care for us. But we see thee, a present deity, not of wood or stone, but real; therefore we pray to thee." It is true that such material-istic and atheistic expressions were probably reprobated by many at the time, as well as by later writers; but the mere possibility of their public enunciation shows how far the Athenians had gone from their old religious beliefs.

Allegorical impersonations, such as that of Antioch, are religious conceptions of a high order compared to this. Nevertheless, one feels that such impersonations can have no separate divine existence apart from the city or the people whom they represent. They are on a different plane of religious belief from Athena, for example, as the goddess of the city. The goddess was, indeed, in some ways representative of what was best in her chosen people; but she was not a mere symbol of its character and its greatness. She existed before it, and would continue though it should disappear from the earth, unlike the Fortune of Antioch, whose very existence was bound up with that of the city she represented.

Another example of personification may be seen in the recumbent figures of river-gods—notably that of the Nile, with his sixteen cubits, as babies, playing around him. River-gods were indeed an object of worship from early times in Greece, and so appear on coins and elsewhere; but this figure of the Nile, a product of Alexandrian art, is not like the earlier gods, who were looked upon as the givers of increase and fertility; it is a mere allegorical impersonation of the river, such as might be made by a modern artist who made no pretence to believe in the existence of such an anthropomorphic river-god. It cannot be counted as religious art at all. And the attributes and accessories of such a figure, the crocodile and hippopotamus, the sphinx and corn and horn of plenty, are all of them symbolic allusions such as are suitable to such a frigid personification. The art of Alexandria is full of such devices ; that of Pergamon is more vigorous and dramatic ; but in both alike we find the influence of a learned study of mythology, full of quaint and far-fetched allusions and symbols. The culmination of this learned mythology is to be seen in the great altar of Pergamon, on which the gods who are in combat with the giants include not only all figures, appropriate and inappropriate, from the Hellenic pantheon, but many other deities whose right of admission to that pantheon is more than doubtful. The figures of the gods no longer correspond to the belief in any real divinities, but are either mere artistic types, repeated again and again in accordance with convention, or else they are regarded as symbols representing different aspects of divine power.

Symbolism of this kind is a common symptom of the decay of religious faith. The more thoughtful or educated classes, who follow the speculations of philosophers as to the nature of the deity, find it possible to reconcile these speculations with the forms of popular religion by accepting the forms in a symbolic sense. The common people, on the other hand, finding the old forms inadequate to satisfy their religious aspirations, import new and strange divinities, whose cult is often mixed with magic or mystic rites. Here, too, the symbols have a meaning other than what appears to the uninitiated eye, and the province of art, which approaches the mind through the senses, is closely circumscribed. A statue or other work of art which needs explanation of its allusions, which does not express an ideal that appeals directly to the imagination of the people, has lost touch with religion, and cannot to any appreciable extent influence it or be influenced by it. The age of idolatry in the higher sense, of a religious imagination that enables the artist to bring the people nearer to their gods, or even the gods nearer to the heart of the people, has passed away, and in its place we find either a superstitious clinging to the magic power of the early objects of worship, or a mere acceptance, as conventional symbols, of forms that bear no direct relation to anything that is believed in as real.

Our brief historical survey has shown us how the Greeks, starting from a belief, such as is common to many primitive religions, in the superhuman powers or sanctity of certain objects, were enabled by their vivid anthropomorphic imagination first to think of the gods as in like form to themselves, and then to make their images in human shape. And as their art progressed towards the power of making a physical type of perfect beauty to serve as the means of expression of this " human form divine," and also to skill in expressing character by means of human features and figures, it became possible for them to embody in their great statues the various ideals of divinity which belonged to their chief gods. Here the skill of the artist would have availed little or nothing if he had not shared with the people for whom he worked a belief in the reality of these ideals, not merely as philosophic aspects of the divine nature, but as real beings who were able to help and to inspire, and to manifest themselves to their worshippers in this human form. The next step is towards an even more vivid realisation of the personality of the gods ; but by bringing them nearer to human level it made the worship of their images less easy to accept in a literal sense to the more thoughtful, while such worship tended, with the common people, to enter upon a more material and less exalted phase. The result was a tendency towards symbolism in which the symbol itself was regarded as a mere convention, and the inspiration and actual communion with men, vouchsafed by the gods through their ideal images, was no longer sought after. When any means of communion between god and man, whether by means of a solemn service or by means of an image which the god himself accepts as his earthly representative, ceases to be felt as anything more than a human device, its religious power must fail. When, on the other hand, we find a union of religion and art to provide a means for this divine intercourse, we may recognise idolatry in its highest form, the use of images not merely as accessories of religious service, but as providing in themselves a channel of worship and inspiration.